Presented to

_____

On the occasion of

_____

From

_____

Date

_____

© 2000 by Barbour Publishing, Inc.

ISBN 1-89306-589-8

Published by Barbour Publishing, Inc., P. O. Box 719, Uhrichsville, Ohio 44683
http://www.barbourbooks.com

 Member of the
Evangelical Christian
Publishers Association

Printed in China.

Homegrown
Heaven Bound

Thoughts on the Fruit of the Spirit

PAUL KENT

FAMILY
CHRISTIAN
PRESS

But the fruit of the Spirit
is love, joy, peace,
patience, kindness, goodness,
faithfulness, gentleness
and self-control.
Against such things
there is no law.
Galatians 5:22–23

*Y*ou love homegrown fruit. So does God.

After months of watering, feeding, weeding, and waiting, there's nothing like the sweet harvest of your own garden. In a similar way, God enjoys the fruits of His labor—the fruit of the Spirit—from the garden of our lives.

So what is the fruit of the Spirit? It's a basketful of Christlike characteristics listed in Galatians 5:22–23—but examples of these traits are found throughout the Bible. Over the centuries, God has cultivated His prized fruit in the lives of His children. He's still doing that today.

Read on for an encouraging collection of Scriptures, poetry, stories, and thoughts that celebrate the fruit of God's Spirit in our lives. Allow the Master Gardener to do His work in your life, and you'll be *Homegrown, Heaven Bound.*

Love

*"By this all men will know that you are my disciples,
if you love one another."*
John 13:35

*H*ow sweet, how heavenly is the sight,
When those who love the Lord
In one another's peace delight,
And so fulfill His Word!

Let love, in one delightful stream,
Through every bosom flow,
And union sweet, and dear esteem,
In every action glow.

Love is the golden chain that binds
The happy souls above;
And he's an heir of heaven who finds
His bosom glow with love.

Joseph Swain

$\mathscr{S}$teadfast love in the midst of adversity. That's the example of Jonathan to his best friend, David. Their friendship arose soon after David's conquest of Goliath; Jonathan, King Saul's son, "loved [David] as himself."

That love would be tested. Jonathan maintained his fidelity to David in spite of his own father's murderous jealousy. Jonathan warned his friend of danger, defended him before the king, and was apparently willing to relinquish his own throne for David.

Jonathan's self-sacrificing love is the kind of love the apostle Paul wrote about in 1 Corinthians 13. The kind of love that's patient, kind, protecting, and never failing. It's the kind of love that, by God's Spirit, should be growing in our lives today.

Brotherly love is still the distinguishing
badge of every true Christian.
Matthew Henry

"My command is this:
Love each other
as I have loved you."
John 15:12

May the Lord make your love increase
and overflow for each other and for everyone else.
1 Thessalonians 3:12

Joy

*"I have told you this so that my joy may be in you
and that your joy may be complete."*
John 15:11

$\mathcal{P}$raise to God, immortal praise,
For the love that crowns our days;
Bounteous Source of every joy,
Let Thy praise our tongues employ.

Flocks that whiten all the plain;
Yellow sheaves of ripened grain;
Clouds that drop their fattening dews,
Suns that temperate warmth diffuse.

These to Thee, my God, we owe,
Source whence all our blessings flow;
And for these my soul shall raise
Grateful vows and solemn praise.

Anna Laetitia Aikin Barbauld

What a day! Harassed by a demon-possessed girl. . .falsely accused . . .stripped and beaten without trial. . .hauled off to prison and fastened into stocks. If that's not enough to elicit a moan of complaint, what is?

But the sounds Paul and Silas made weren't whines of protest. They were hymns of praise. As midnight approached, they were praying and singing and expressing a joy that only God could provide. It's the same kind of joy—a deep spiritual joy, independent of circumstances—that God will provide us as His Spirit develops its fruit in our lives.

Our faith will land few of us in prison. But the joy that Paul and Silas showed there can be ours, too—in whatever trials we face.

One inch of joy surmounts of grief a span,
Because to laugh is proper to the man.
Francis Rabelais

"The joy of the LORD is your strength."
Nehemiah 8:10

You have made known to me the path of life;
you will fill me with joy in your presence,
with eternal pleasures at your right hand.
Psalm16:11

Peace

"I have told you these things, so that in me you may have peace.
In this world you will have trouble.
But take heart! I have overcome the world."
John 16:33

*P*eace, perfect peace, in this dark world of sin?
The blood of Jesus whispers peace within.

Peace, perfect peace, by thronging duties pressed?
To do the will of Jesus, this is rest.

Peace, perfect peace, with sorrows surging round?
On Jesus' bosom naught but calm is found.

Peace, perfect peace, our future all unknown?
Jesus we know, and He is on the throne.

Peace, perfect peace, death shadowing us and ours?
Jesus has vanquished death and all its powers.

It is enough: earth's struggles soon shall cease,
And Jesus call us to heaven's perfect peace.

Edward Henry Bickersteth, Jr.

$\mathscr{T}$he idea was shocking and fraught with implications. How would her family and friends respond to an unmarried young woman's pregnancy? What would her fiancé think? Could she really be the one to carry and give birth to the Son of God?

When God's messenger first appeared with the news, Mary felt fear. But soon, with the angel's assurance of God's favor, she was able to say, "I am the Lord's servant. May it be to me as you have said." And with that simple, composed reaction, she began a journey that would change the world forever.

In this sinful world, peace is not a natural element in our lives. But it will arise supernaturally, as God's Spirit does His work inside us.

From toil he wins his spirits light,
from busy day the peaceful night.
Rich, from the very want of wealth,
In heaven's best treasures, peace and health.
Thomas Gray

Great peace have
they who love your law.
Psalm 119:165

You will keep in perfect peace
him whose mind is steadfast,
because he trusts in you.
Isaiah 26:3

Patience

Knowing this, that the trying of your faith worketh patience.
But let patience have her perfect work,
that ye may be perfect and entire, wanting nothing.
James 1:3–4, KJV

Slow to anger, full of kindness,
Rich in mercy, Lord, Thou art,
Wash me in Thy healing fountain,
Take away my sinful heart.

May Thy ever gracious spirit,
Lead me in the way of truth,
May I learn the voice of wisdom,
In the early days of youth.

Fanny Crosby

$\mathcal{M}$aybe you've heard of "the patience of Job." Thousands of years after he lived, Job is still the standard of patient endurance. And why not? He bore up under the most crushing load imaginable.

In a brief period of time, Job lost his children, his possessions, and his health. Then, for some time, he endured three accusing "friends" who argued that his own sin had caused his problems. And though he certainly struggled, Job maintained his belief in God, rejecting his faithless wife's advice to "curse God and die."

We can pray that we never face the trials that Job faced. But for the difficulties life sends our way, God promises the Spirit-fruit of patience. "Better a patient man than a warrior," said Solomon, "a man who controls his temper than one who takes a city" (Proverbs 16:32).

Be patient, then, brothers, until the Lord's coming.
See how the farmer waits for the land to yield its valuable crop,
and how patient he is for the autumn and spring rains.
James 5:7

Patience is the best remedy for every trouble.
Plautus

I waited patiently for the LORD;
he turned to me and heard my cry.
Psalm 40:1

Kindness

*Make sure that nobody pays back wrong for wrong,
but always try to be kind to each other
and to everyone else.*
1 Thessalonians 5:15

$\mathcal{D}$o good unto others, do good while we can,
Our moments how quickly they fly;
Remember the proverb, remember it now,
We all can do good if we try.

A look or a smile, that kindness we give,
May comfort a desolate heart;
May sweeten a life that is lonely and sad,
And hope to the weary impart

Fanny Crosby

$\mathscr{B}$eaten and bloodied, a man lay half-dead along the roadway. He had been attacked by robbers, who took what they wanted and left their victim at the mercy of whatever other travelers might happen by.

Unfortunately for the sufferer, the first two passersby—holy men, ironically—didn't want to get involved. They stepped around the man and continued on their way. But the next traveler, a man of another race, showed a kindness that shines as a beacon through the centuries. This man demonstrated a self-sacrificing helpfulness that Jesus used to define the word "neighbor" for those who couldn't grasp the concept of "love your neighbor as yourself."

The story, of course, is that of the Good Samaritan. The point, for those developing the fruit of the Spirit in their lives, is to "Go and do likewise" (Luke 10:37).

Little deeds of kindness, little words of love,
Help to make earth happy like the heaven above.
Julie Fletcher

Be kind and compassionate
to one another,
forgiving each other,
just as in Christ God forgave you.
Ephesians 4:32

Therefore, as God's chosen people, holy and dearly loved,
clothe yourselves with. . .kindness.
Colossians 3:12

Goodness

*And we pray this in order that you may live a life
worthy of the Lord and may please him in every way;
bearing fruit in every good work.*
Colossians 1:10

*P*urer in heart, O God, help me to be;
May I devote my life wholly to Thee:
Watch Thou my wayward feet,
Guide me with counsel sweet;
Purer in heart, help me to be.

Purer in heart, O God, help me to be;
Until Thy holy face one day I see:
Keep me from secret sin,
Reign Thou my soul within;
Purer in heart, help me to be.

Fannie Estelle Davison

The people just couldn't understand. When had their King ever been in prison? When had He needed food, or drink, or clothing, or companionship? And why was He commending them for providing all of those things to Him?

The enigmatic story was one of Jesus' parables, told to His disciples shortly before His arrest and crucifixion. The explanation, Jesus said, was that whatever good deeds the people had done for "the least of these brothers of mine" had been done for the King himself—God.

Goodness—compassion, generosity, and service—should always be growing in our lives, as an indicator of the fruit of God's Spirit. How are we treating "the least of these brothers of mine" (Matthew 25:40)?

Goodness does not consist in greatness,
but greatness in goodness.
Athenaeus

In everything, set them an example by doing what is good.
Titus 2:7

Live such good lives among the pagans that,
though they accuse you of doing wrong, they may see
your good deeds and glorify God
on the day he visits us.
1 Peter 2:12

Faithfulness

Now it is required that those
who have been given a trust must prove faithful.
1 Corinthians 4:2

*A*m I a soldier of the cross,
A follower of the Lamb,
And shall I fear to own His cause,
Or blush to speak His Name?

Are there no foes for me to face?
Must I not stem the flood?
Is this vile world a friend to grace,
To help me on to God?

Sure I must fight if I would reign;
Increase my courage, Lord.
I'll bear the toil, endure the pain,
Supported by Thy Word.

Isaac Watts

Nehemiah had a big job to do. He felt the Lord's urging to rebuild the walls of Jerusalem, and he tackled the work with vigor. And when troubles arose, Nehemiah turned to God for the strength to overcome them.

First, he encouraged his workers to ignore the ridicule their enemies heaped upon them. Then he organized armed guards to protect the wall builders as they worked—in fact, the Scripture says Nehemiah carried his weapon even when going for water, and his laborers carried materials in one hand and a weapon in the other. Finally, Nehemiah defused a troubling situation in which the noblemen and officials of the Jews were taking advantage of the wall builders through high-interest loans.

Difficult situations all, but each was handled faithfully by a godly man named Nehemiah. Our trials will certainly be different than Nehemiah's, but our faithfulness should be growing every day to accomplish the tasks that God places before us.

A faithful and good servant is a real godsend;
but truly 'tis a rare bird in the land.
Martin Luther

"Be faithful. . .
and I will give you
the crown of life."
Revelation 2:10

A faithful man will be richly blessed.
Proverbs 28:20

Gentleness

Let your gentleness be evident to all.
Philippians 4:5

Father, make us loving, gentle, thoughtful, kind;
Fill us with Thy Spirit, make us of Thy mind.
Help us love each other, more and more each day,
Help us follow Jesus, in the narrow way.

Refrain
We would learn of Jesus,
Help us here below,
Follow in His footsteps,
Who hath loved us so.

Help us to remember, Thou art ever near;
Teach us lovingkindness, tenderness and cheer.
There is much of sorrow, in this world below;
Father, make us loving, Thou hast loved us so.

Flora Kirkland

$\mathcal{R}$ead through the Gospels, and you'll get the impression that Jesus really enjoyed children. Matthew, Mark, and Luke all relate the story of crowds bringing their babies and little children to Jesus for His blessing. The disciples, concerned with weightier matters, scolded the parents for wasting Jesus' time, but Jesus in turn scolded the disciples: "Let the little children come to me, and do not hinder them, for the kingdom of God belongs to such as these."

Jesus not only prayed over the children, he put His hands on them, and, according to Mark, took them into His arms. The Son of God was a rough-hewn carpenter, a person of the outdoors, a man who could physically remove money-changers from the temple. But He was also the picture of gentleness, especially with the weakest members of society. As His Spirit works in our lives, we'll show that gentleness to others, as well.

Self-Control

Be self-controlled and alert. Your enemy, the devil,
prowls around like a roaring lion looking for someone to devour.
1 Peter 5:8

*S*o let our lips and lives express
The holy gospel we profess;
So let our works and virtues shine,
To prove the doctrine all divine.

Thus shall we best proclaim abroad
The honors of our Savior God,
When the salvation reigns within,
And grace subdues the power of sin.

Our flesh and sense must be denied,
Passion and envy, lust and pride;
While justice, temp'rance, truth, and love,
Our inward piety approve.

Isaac Watts

$\mathcal{R}$emember the story of Joseph? As the youngest, most favored, of Jacob's twelve sons, Joseph incurred the anger of his brothers, who sold him into slavery. God blessed Joseph, though, and he ultimately became an important aide in the house of the Egyptian officer Potiphar.

The Bible notes that Joseph was "well built and handsome," and he soon caught the eye of Potiphar's wife. It's very possible that she, as the wife of a power national official, was also good-looking; certainly, she was wealthy and powerful. A Hollywood writer would bring this couple together into a passionate relationship—but in reality, Joseph knew that any involvement with Potiphar's wife would be seriously wrong. Even though she tried to force herself on him, he chose to run away.

That's self-control. And it's an evidence of the fruit of God's Spirit. Joseph didn't run from temptation to maintain his own reputation, or to protect Potiphar's wife, or for any reason other than the question he posed to her: "How then could I do such a wicked thing and sin against God?"

So how does your garden grow? Is the fruit of God's Spirit developing, slowly but surely, in your life? It's a long process, certainly—but take heart in every small victory, every act of love, joy, peace, patience, kindness, goodness, faithfulness, gentleness, or self-control you experience. It's a sign that Jesus Christ, the Master Gardener, is guiding you toward a beautiful harvest.

Lord, thank You for working
in the garden of my soul.
May my harvest be bountiful,
for You and the people around me.